The Scale of
BUILDINGS & STRUCTURES

Joanna Brundle
Crabtree Publishing Company
www.crabtreebooks.com

CRABTREE
PUBLISHING COMPANY
WWW.CRABTREEBOOKS.COM

Author: Joanna Brundle

Editorial director: Kathy Middleton

Editors: Emilie Dufresne, Janine Deschenes

Design: Jasmine Pointer

Proofreader: Crystal Sikkens

Prepress technician: Tammy McGarr

Print coordinator: Katherine Berti

All facts, statistics, web addresses and URLs in this book were
verified as valid and accurate at time of writing.
No responsibility for any changes to external websites or
references can be accepted by either the author or publisher.

Image Credits

All images courtesy of Shutterstock.com. With
thanks to Getty Images, Thinkstock Photo and
iStockphoto.

Front Cover – Boyko.Pictures, gst. 2–3 – Malika Keehl.
4–5 – KittyVector. 6–7 – Naty_Lee, NotionPic, Tako
design. 8–9 – Tako design, larry laurence marcelo,
twins_nika, rorrak. 10–11 – Champ008, MatoomMi,
BILEY-16. 12–13 – Walking-onstreet, vberla.
14–15 – Merfin. 16–17 – Red monkey, ONYXprj,
studioworkstock, Zarica. 18–19 – Fay Francevna,
Rattanamanee Patpong. 20–21 – ProStockStudio.

Library and Archives Canada Cataloguing in Publication

Title: The scale of buildings & structures / Joanna Brundle.
Other titles: Scale of buildings and structures
Names: Brundle, Joanna, author.
Description: Series statement: The scale of things |
   Previously published: King's Lynn, Norfolk : BookLife Publishing, 2019. |
   Includes index.
Identifiers: Canadiana (print) 2019019183X | Canadiana (ebook) 20190191848
   ISBN 9780778776543 (hardcover) |
   ISBN 9780778776604 (softcover) |
   ISBN 9781427125262 (HTML)
Subjects: LCSH: Tall buildings—Juvenile literature. | LCSH: Skyscrapers—
   Juvenile literature. | LCSH: Measurement—Juvenile literature. |
   LCSH: Size perception—Juvenile literature. | LCSH: Size judgment—
   Juvenile literature.
Classification: LCC NA6230 .B78 2020 | DDC j720/.483—dc23

Library of Congress Cataloging-in-Publication Data

Names: Brundle, Joanna, author.
Title: The scale of buildings and structures / Joanna Brundle.
Description: New York : Crabtree Publishing Company, [2019] |
   Series: The scale of things | Includes index.
Identifiers: LCCN 2019043936 (print) | LCCN 2019043937 (ebook) |
   ISBN 9780778776543 (hardcover) |
   ISBN 9780778776604 (paperback) |
   ISBN 9781427125262 (ebook)
Subjects: LCSH: Buildings--Juvenile literature. | Weights and measures--
   Juvenile literature.
Classification: LCC TH149 .B78 2019 (print) | LCC TH149 (ebook) |
   DDC 720--dc23
LC record available at https://lccn.loc.gov/2019043936
LC ebook record available at https://lccn.loc.gov/2019043937

Crabtree Publishing Company

www.crabtreebooks.com   1–800–387–7650
Published by Crabtree Publishing Company in 2020

©2019 BookLife Publishing Ltd.

Printed in the U.S.A./012020/CG20191115

Published in Canada
Crabtree Publishing
616 Welland Ave.
St. Catharines, Ontario
L2M 5V6

Published in the United States
Crabtree Publishing
PMB 59051
350 Fifth Avenue, 59th Floor
New York, New York 10118

CONTENTS

Words that are in **bold** can

INTRODUCTION

The scale of things means how one thing compares in size to another. In this book, we will compare famous buildings and **structures** by how tall they are. A building is a type of structure that humans use to meet a **need**, such as shelter or a place to work.

Height is a measurement **of how tall something is.**

Some famous buildings and structures are less than 200 feet (60 m) tall. Others are thousands of feet (hundreds of meters) tall. Some measurements in this book are **approximate**. You can read the measurements that match the ones you learn in school.

We will measure **the heights of different buildings in feet and meters (m). A door in your house or school is around 6.5 feet (2 m) tall. A regular telephone pole is around 35 feet (10.6 m) tall. Use these measurements to help you imagine how tall these structures are.**

THE COLOSSEUM AND THE LEANING TOWER OF PISA

The Colosseum is the largest **amphitheater** in the world. Inside, huge crowds of people watched **gladiators** fight one another. The Colosseum is in Rome, Italy.

The Colosseum is about 157 feet (48 m) tall.

157 feet (48 m)

28 feet (9 m)

157 feet (48 m)

187 feet (57 m)

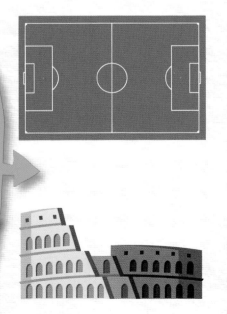

A soccer field could easily fit inside the Colosseum. There was room for around 50,000 people.

The Leaning Tower of Pisa is about 187 feet (57 m) tall. That's around the same height as the Colosseum, plus the height of two double decker buses.

14 feet (4.3 m)

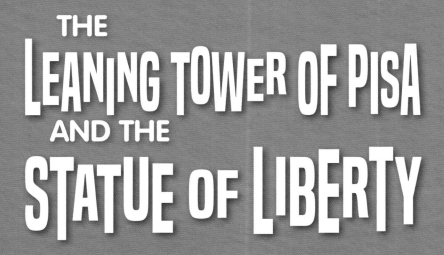

THE LEANING TOWER OF PISA AND THE STATUE OF LIBERTY

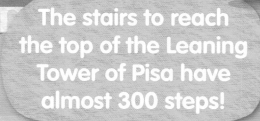

The stairs to reach the top of the Leaning Tower of Pisa have almost 300 steps!

The Leaning Tower of Pisa is famous for the way it leans to one side. But did you know that it was built standing straight? The tower started leaning over time because it was built on soft soil. One side of the tower sunk into the soil.

The Statue of Liberty is about 305 feet (93 m) tall. That's as tall as the Leaning Tower of Pisa, with eight double decker buses stacked on top.

305 feet (93 m)

112 feet (34.4 m)

187 feet (57 m)

x 101

The Statue of Liberty is also about the same height as the Leaning Tower of Pisa, plus 101 large pizzas, side by side.

THE STATUE OF LIBERTY AND THE LONDON EYE

The statue's sandals are 25 feet (7.6 m) long. That would make her shoe size 879!

The Statue of Liberty stands on Liberty Island in New York Harbor. The statue is a **symbol** of freedom. The statue carries a torch. The flame is covered in **gold leaf**.

305 feet (93 m)

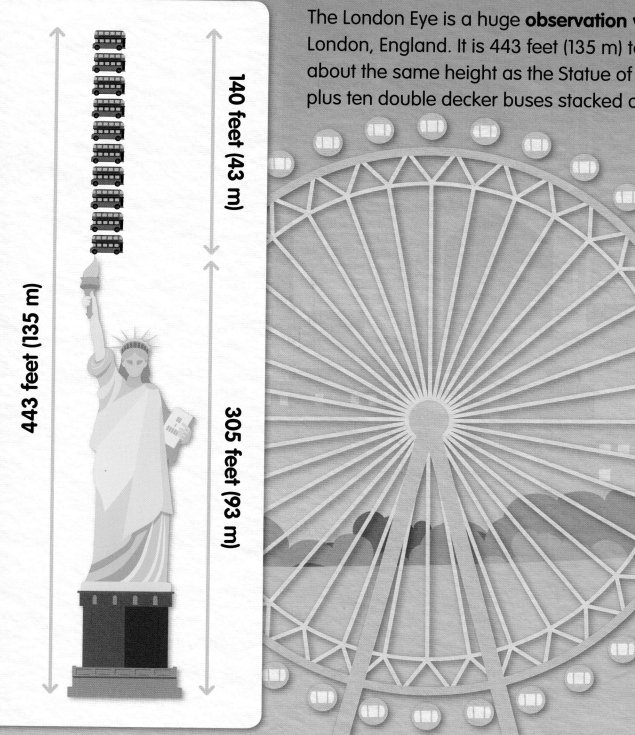

The London Eye is a huge **observation wheel** in London, England. It is 443 feet (135 m) tall. That's about the same height as the Statue of Liberty, plus ten double decker buses stacked on top.

140 feet (43 m)

443 feet (135 m)

305 feet (93 m)

443 feet (135 m)

THE LONDON EYE AND THE GOLDEN GATE BRIDGE

The London Eye is nearly 200 TIMES larger than the wheel of an adult's bicycle.

pod

There are 32 pods on the London Eye. Up to 28 people stand in each pod. They can view London in all directions. On sunny days, people can see up to 25 miles (40 km) away.

The famous Golden Gate Bridge is in San Francisco, California. Its towers rise 746 feet (227 m) above the water. That's almost as tall as the London Eye and the Statue of Liberty joined together!

746 feet (227 m)

305 feet (93 m)

443 feet (135 m)

746 feet (227 m)

THE GOLDEN GATE BRIDGE AND THE EIFFEL TOWER

The Golden Gate Bridge crosses a stretch of water called the Golden Gate. It connects the city of San Francisco with other areas of California. Millions of people visit it each year.

More than 100,000 vehicles cross the bridge every day.

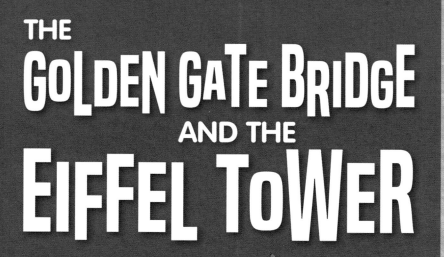

305 feet (93 m)

1,063 feet (324 m)

746 feet (227 m)

The Eiffel Tower in Paris, France, is 1,063 feet (324 m) tall. That's taller than the Golden Gate Bridge and the Statue of Liberty joined together.

THE EIFFEL TOWER AND THE EMPIRE STATE BUILDING

The Eiffel Tower is named after Gustave Eiffel. He was the **engineer** who designed it. The tower was built in 1889. At night, the tower is lit up by 20,000 light bulbs!

Visitors can climb 674 steps to reach the tower's second floor. That is like climbing a staircase in a house about 50 times.

The Empire State Building in New York City is 1,454 feet (443 m) tall. That's taller than the Eiffel Tower with two Leaning Towers of Pisa stacked on top of it.

374 feet (114 m)

1,063 feet (324 m)

1,454 feet (443 m)

THE EMPIRE STATE BUILDING AND SHANGHAI TOWER

The Empire State Building has 103 floors, with 1,860 steps up to the 102nd floor. Visitors enjoy amazing views of New York City from there.

187 feet (57 m)

443 feet (135 m)

1,454 feet (443 m)

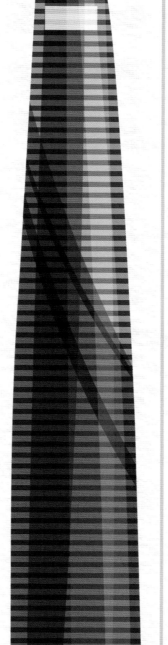

2,073 feet (632 m)

Shanghai Tower is a mega-tall tower in Shanghai, China. Its full height is 2,073 feet (632 m). That's almost as tall as the Empire State Building, the London Eye, and the Leaning Tower of Pisa stacked on top of each other.

SHANGHAI TOWER AND BURJ KHALIFA

An **observation deck** on the 118th floor of Shanghai Tower gives amazing views of the city. To get there, visitors take one of the fastest elevators in the world!

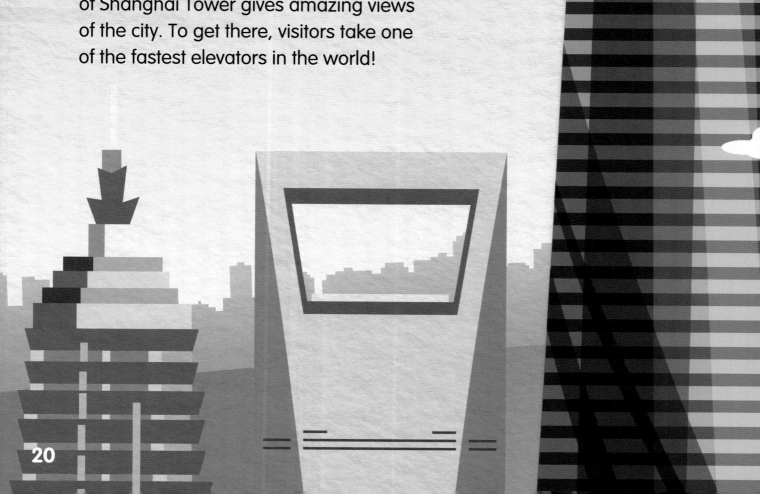

At 2,717 feet (828 m) tall, the Burj Khalifa in Dubai is the world's tallest building. It is taller than Shanghai Tower, the London Eye, and the Leaning Tower of Pisa stacked on top of each other.

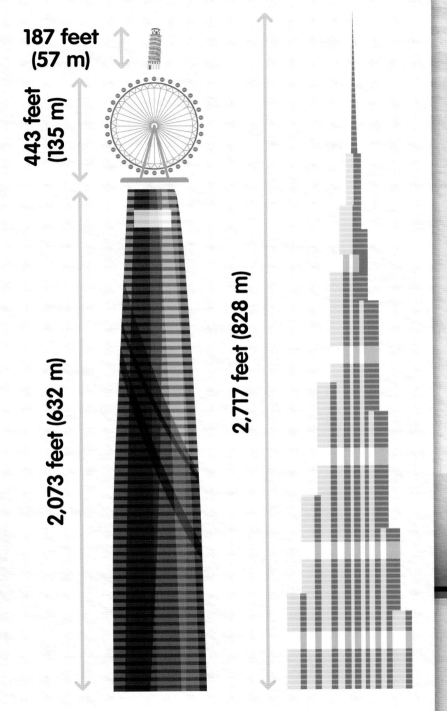

187 feet (57 m)

443 feet (135 m)

2,073 feet (632 m)

2,717 feet (828 m)

BURJ KHALIFA

The Burj Khalifa has more than 160 floors. Inside, there are restaurants, offices, **apartments**, and a hotel. It broke many **records**, including having the highest number of floors and the highest outdoor observation deck.

Not usable

Usable

When it opened in 2010, the Burj Khalifa easily broke the record for the world's tallest building. But taller and taller structures are being planned. The Burj Khalifa may not keep its record forever!

Just two-thirds of the Burj Khalifa can be used by people. The rest was added only to make the building taller.

GLOSSARY

amphitheater An open, round theater with curved rows that rise from the center stage

apartment A home made up of a room or set of rooms in a building

approximate Close to an exact measurement

engineer A person who uses math, science, and creative thinking to design or improve something

gladiators Men trained to fight at shows in ancient Roman

gold leaf A very thin sheet of gold that can be placed over things

measure Find out the size or amount of something

measurement The number we get after measuring something

need Something that a person requires

observation deck A viewing place in a tall building

observation wheel A large, rotating wheel with passenger cars attached to it, allowing people to ride safely and enjoy a view

record The known and recorded, or written-down, facts about something

structures Human-built objects, made of different parts that are put together

symbol Something that represents something else

INDEX